THE
OF O

IMMORTAL LE

THE MAGIC OF POSITIV

CHRISTIAN D. LARSON
The Optimist Creed

CLAUDE M. BRISTOL
The Magic of Believing

FLORENCE SCOVEL SHINN
The Secret Door to Success

A.H.Z. CARR
How to Attract Good Luck

ABRIDGED AND INTRODUCED BY
MITCH HOROWITZ

Published by Gildan Media LLC
aka G&D Media.
www.GandDmedia.com

The Optimist Creed originally appeared in Christian D. Larson's book *Your Forces and How to Use Them* (1910)
The Magic of Believing was originally published in 1948
The Secret Door to Success was originally published in 1940
How to Attract Good Luck was originally published in 1952
G&D Media Condensed Classics editions published 2019

FIRST EDITION: 2019

Cover design by David Rheinhardt of Pyrographx

Interior design by Meghan Day Healey of Story Horse, LLC.

ISBN: 978-1-7225-0203-4

Contents

Introduction
vii

THE OPTIMIST CREED
1

THE MAGIC OF BELIEVING
5

THE SECRET DOOR TO SUCCESS
57

HOW TO ATTRACT GOOD LUCK
113

Introduction

The Power of *Maybe*

By Mitch Horowitz

Does optimism or self-belief matter? Does it really change anything—or does it, as some critics says, put us at risk of dangerous self-delusion? Any kind of thinking taken to an extreme can result in delusion. But without a sturdy sense of self-belief, nothing is possible—and nothing will be there to rescue you when faced with challenges or urgencies.

Indeed, remarkable things can emerge from a feeling of fresh possibility and optimism. American philosopher William James called it the sense of "maybe." He wrote this in his 1895 essay *Is Life Worth Living?*:

> *The "scientific" life itself has much to do with maybes, and human life at large has everything to do with them. So far as man stands for anything, and is productive or originative at all, his entire vital function may be said to be to deal with maybes. Not a victory is gained, not a deed*

> *of faithfulness or courage is done, except upon a maybe . . . It is only by risking our persons from one hour to another that we live at all. And often enough our faith beforehand in an uncertified result* is the only thing that makes the result come true. *Suppose, for instance, that you are climbing a mountain and have worked yourself into a position from which the only escape is by a terrible leap. Have faith that you can successfully make it, and your feet are nerved to its accomplishment. But mistrust yourself, and think of all the sweet things you have heard the scientists say of* maybes, *and you will hesitate so that, at last, all unstrung and trembling, and launching yourself in a moment of despair, you roll in the abyss. In such a case . . . the part of wisdom as well as of courage is to* believe what is in the line of your needs, *for only by the belief is the need fulfilled.*

James saw *belief* in something as the determining factor as to how or whether you experience its effects. Hence, belief in a desired outcome can, in itself, increase its possibility via the tools and applications needed to bring it about.

It is in this vein that I invite you to enter this volume of condensed works on the power of optimism.

I hope you enter it with a sense of adventure. These are not myopic works. They are works for the strong-minded. Works for people who know where they are—and where they want to be. And for people who believe, quite rightly, that the power of thought is a vital component to arriving.

The Optimist Creed

THE OPTIMIST CREED

Promise Yourself...

To be so strong that nothing can disturb your peace of mind.

To talk health, happiness and prosperity to every person you meet.

To make all your friends feel that there is something in them.

To look at the sunny side of everything and make your optimism come true.

To think only of the best, to work only for the best, and to expect only the best.

To be just as enthusiastic about the success of others as you are about your own.

To forget the mistakes of the past and press on to the greater achievements of the future.

To wear a cheerful countenance at all times and give every living creature you meet a smile.

To give so much time to the improvement of yourself that you have no time to criticize others.

To be too large for worry, too noble for anger, too strong for fear, and too happy to permit the presence of trouble.

To think well of yourself and to proclaim this fact to the world, not in loud words, but in great deeds.

To live in the faith that the whole world is on your side, so long as you are true to the best that is in you.

The Magic of Believing

Contents

Introduction
The Metaphysics of Success 11

Chapter One
How I Came to Tap the Power of Belief 15

Chapter Two
Mind-Stuff Experiments 17

Chapter Three
Suggestion Is Power 27

Chapter Four
The Art of Mental Pictures 31

Chapter Five
The Mirror Technique for Releasing the Subconscious 35

CHAPTER SIX
How to Project Your Thoughts 41

CHAPTER SEVEN
Belief Makes Things Happen 51

ABOUT THE AUTHORS 55

Introduction

The Metaphysics of Success

By Mitch Horowitz

The American metaphysical scene has produced no other figure quite like Claude M. Bristol. Born in 1891, Bristol had a background as varied as the nation itself: a veteran, a seeker, a sometime journalist, a sometime businessman, and an enthusiast of the possibilities and powers of the mind.

As a veteran, Bristol returned from World War One to witness a nation in transition. The American economy was growing but the mass of people returning from the war, many of whom came from agrarian roots and had never worked in manufacturing or large offices, were unsure of how to enter the new economy. Bristol believed that the threshold of prosperity began in the mind. He wrote his two and only books—the fullest being *The Magic of Believing*—in order to place his ideas about the powers of the mind within reach of the broadest range of people.

Within this abridgement of his immensely popular book you're going to hear about topics that are not always held in high repute these days: ESP, telepathy, and telekinesis, among them. When abridging this book, I made the decision to retain this material—and I did not do so lightly. As I've written in my own analysis of the positive-thinking movement, *One Simple Idea*, I believe that many journalists and academics today have failed to understand, or even attain basic familiarity with, the experiments to which Bristol refers, particularly those conducted by ESP researcher J.B. Rhine at Duke University beginning in the early 1930s.

I take seriously Bristol's contention that legitimate parapsychology has much to offer the motivational seeker. Speaking as a historian who has considered this field, I can vouch for the general validity of Bristol's popularizations and suggested applications of some parapsychological experiments. Indeed, Bristol was one of the few positive-mind theorists of his day who rightly highlighted the work of J.B. Rhine and his contemporaries.

I think that you will find *The Magic of Believing*, first published in 1948, a surprising and still-radical journey into the possibilities of the mind. We remain at the early stages of grappling with higher mental possibilities today, gaining a glimpse of them in a new wave of experiments in placebo studies, neuroplasticity, precognition, and quantum theorizing.

Bristol, in his way, makes very large questions about the mind seem simple—because he believed that simple, personal experiments *were* possible, and could prove the efficacy of positive-mind mechanics in daily life, including in matters of career, creativity, and relationships.

I think Bristol was right. And I invite you to approach this book with a spirit of enthusiasm, expectancy, and personal adventure.

Chapter One

How I Came to Tap the Power of Belief

Is there a something, a force, a factor, a power, a science—call it what you will—which a few people understand and use to overcome their difficulties and achieve outstanding success? I firmly believe that there is, and it is my purpose to attempt to explain it so that you may use it if you desire.

About fifteen years ago the financial editor of a great Los Angeles newspaper, after attending lectures I had given to financial men in that city, wrote: "You have caught from the ether something that has a mystical quality—a something that explains the magic of coincidence, the mystery of what makes men lucky."

I realized that I had run across something that was workable, but I didn't consider it then, neither do I now, as anything mystical, except in the sense that it is unknown to the majority of people. It is something that has always been known to a fortunate few down the centuries, but, for some unknown reason, is little understood by the average person.

When I started out years ago to teach this science, I wasn't certain that it could be or would be grasped by the ordinary individual; but now that I have seen those who have used it double and triple their incomes, build their own successful businesses, acquire homes in the country, and create sizable fortunes, I am convinced that any intelligent person who is sincere with himself can reach any heights he desires.

The science of thought is as old as man himself. The wise men of all ages have known about it and used it. The only thing the writer has done is to put the subject in modern language and bring to the reader's attention what a few of the outstanding minds of today are doing to substantiate the great truths that have come down through the centuries.

Much has been written and said about mystical powers, unknown forces, the occult, metaphysics, mental physics, psychology, black and white magic, and many kindred subjects, causing most people to believe that they are in the field of the supernatural. Perhaps they are for some, but my conclusion is that the only inexplicable thing about these powers is that it is *belief* that makes them work.

Chapter Two

Mind-Stuff Experiments

In order to get a clearer understanding of our subject, the reader should give thought to thought itself and to its phenomena. No one knows what thought really is, other than it is some sort of mental action; but, like the unknown element electricity, we see its manifestations everywhere. We see it in the actions and expressions of a child, in an aged person, in animals, and, in fact, to varying degrees in every living thing. The more we contemplate and study thought, the more we realize what a terrific force it is and how unlimited are its powers.

Glance around as you read this. If you are in a furnished room, your eyes tell you that you are looking at a number of inanimate objects. That is true so far as visual perception is concerned; but in reality you are actually looking at thoughts or ideas that have come into materialization through the creative work of some human being. It was a thought, first, that created the furniture, fashioned the window glass, gave form to the draperies and coverings.

The automobile, the skyscraper, the great planes that sweep the stratosphere, the sewing machine, the tiny pin, a thousand and one things—yes, millions of objects—where did they come from originally? Only one source. From that strange force— thought. As we analyze further, we realize that these achievements, and in fact all of our possessions, came as a result of creative thinking. Ralph Waldo Emerson declared that the ancestor of every action is thought; when we understand that, we begin to comprehend that our world is governed by thought and that everything without had its counterpart originally within the mind. It is just as Buddha said many centuries ago: "All that we are is the result of what we have thought."

Figuratively, thought makes giants out of pigmies, and often turns giants into pigmies. History is filled with accounts of how thought has made weak men strong and strong men weak, and we see evidence of its working around us constantly.

You do not eat, wear clothes, run for a bus, drive your automobile, go for a walk, or read a newspaper—you don't even raise your arm—without a preceding thought-impulse. While you may consider the motions you make as more or less automatic, perhaps caused by some physical reflexes, behind every single step you take in life, regardless of its direction, is that formidable and powerful force—thought.

The very way you walk, the way you carry yourself, your talk, your manner of dress, all reflect your way of thinking. A slovenly carriage is an indication of slovenly thinking, whereas an alert, upright carriage is the outward sign of inward strength and confidence. What you exhibit outwardly, you are inwardly.

You are the product of your own thought. What you believe yourself to be, you are.

Thought is the original source of all wealth, all success, all material gain, all great discoveries and inventions, and of all achievement. Without it there would be no great empires, no great fortunes, no great transcontinental rail lines, no modern conveniences; in fact, there would be no advance over life in the most primitive ages.

Your thoughts, those that predominate, determine your character, your career, indeed your everyday life. Thus it becomes easy to understand what is meant by the statement that a man's thoughts make or break him. And when we realize that there can be no action or reaction, either good or bad, without the generating force of thought initiating it, the Biblical saying, "For whatsoever a man soweth, that shall he also reap," and Shakespeare's words, "There is nothing either good or bad, but thinking makes it so," become more intelligible.

Sir Arthur Eddington, the English physicist, says that to an altogether unsuspected extent the universe in which we live is a creation of our minds; while the late Sir James Jeans, who was equally famous in the same field, suggested that the universe was merely a creation that resulted from the thought of some great universal mind underlying and coordinating all of our minds. Nothing is clearer than that the world's greatest scientists and thinkers of our age are not only voicing the ideas of the wisest men of old, but that they are confirming the fundamental principle of this book.

Almost since the beginning of the human race, the molding of men has been done by those who knew something of thought's great power. All the great religious leaders, kings, warriors, statesmen have understood this science and have known that people act as they think and also react to the thought of others, especially when it is stronger and more convincing than their own. Accordingly, men of powerful dynamic thought have ever swayed the people by appealing to their minds, sometimes to lead them into freedom and sometimes into slavery. There never was a period in history when we should study our own thoughts more, try to understand them, and learn how to use them to improve our position in life, by drawing upon the great source of power that lies within each of us.

There was a time when I would have laughed at people who talked about the magnetic force of thought, how thought correlates with its object, how it can affect people and inanimate things, even at great distances. But I no longer laugh, nor do others who know something of its power, for anyone who has any intelligence sooner or later comes to the realization that thought can change the surface of the entire globe.

The late George Russell, famous Irish editor and poet, was quoted as saying that we become what we contemplate. Undoubtedly, we become what we envisage, and he certainly demonstrated it in his own life by becoming a great writer, lecturer, painter, and poet.

However, it must be borne in mind that many of our ideas, the thoughts we think, are not ours at all, or those of our own originating. We are molded also by the thoughts of others; by what we hear in our social life, what we read in newspapers, magazines, and books; what we hear in the movies, the theater, and on the radio; even by chance remarks from the conversation of bystanders—and these thoughts bombard us constantly. Some of them that accord with our own inmost thoughts and also open the way to greater visions in our life are helpful. But often there are thoughts that are upsetting, that weaken our self-confidence, and turn us away from our high purposes. It is these outside thoughts that are the troublemakers, and later I shall point out how you can keep free of them.

One essential to success is that your desire be an all-obsessing one, your thoughts and aims be coordinated, and your energy be concentrated and applied without letup. It may be riches or fame or position or knowledge that you want, for each person has his own idea of what success means to him. But whatever you consider it to be, you can have it provided you are willing to make the objective the burning desire of your life. A big order, you say. Not at all; by using the dynamic force of believing, you can set all your inner forces in motion, and they in turn will help you to reach your goal. If you are married, you remember the stimulating and emotional experience of courting the girl you wanted for your wife. Certainly, it wasn't nerve-racking work—quite the contrary, you'll admit—but what were you using, if not this very same science, even though unconsciously. The desire to win a helpmate was uppermost in your mind from the time you got the idea until your marriage. The thought, the belief, was with you every minute of the day and perhaps it was with you in your dreams.

Now that you have a clearer idea of the part that thought and desire play in our daily lives, the first thing to determine is precisely what you want. Starting in with the general idea that you merely want to be a success, as most people do, is too indefinite. You must have a mental pattern clearly drawn in your mind. Ask yourself: Where am I headed? What is my goal? Have I visualized just what I really want? If success is to be measured in terms of wealth, can you fix the amount in figures? If in terms of achievement, can you specify it definitely?

I ask these questions, for in their answers are factors that will determine your whole life from now on. Strange as it may appear, not one out of a hundred people can answer these questions. Most people have a general idea that they would like to be a success, but beyond that everything is vague. They merely go along from day to day figuring that if they have a job today they will have it tomorrow, and that somehow they will be looked after in their old age. They are like a cork on the water floating aimlessly, drawn this way and that by various currents, and either being washed up on the shore, or becoming waterlogged and eventually sinking.

Therefore, it is vital that you know exactly what you want out of life. You must know where you are headed, and you must keep a fixed goal in view. That, of course, is the over-all picture; it makes no difference whether you want *a* job or a *better* one, a new house, a place in the country, or just a new pair of shoes. You must have a fixed idea before you'll obtain what you are after.

There is a great difference between a need and a desire. For example, you may *need* a new car for business, and you may *desire* one in order to give pleasure to your family. The one for your business you will get as a matter of necessity. The one for your family you will plan to get as soon as possible. For this car you will make an extra effort, because it is something you have never had before, something that will add to your responsibilities, and something that will compel you to seek new powers within yourself and new resources outside. It is desire for something new, something different, something that is going to change your life, that causes you to make an extra effort; and it is the *power of believing* that alone sets in motion those inner forces by which you add what I call *plus-values* to your life.

Do you know that departments of psychology in great universities have already undertaken experiments to determine whether the mind possesses the power to influence material objects, and that the experiments have already demonstrated the existence of such a power? While the experiments have not been too widely publicized, there have been stories appearing from time to time giving the general facts.

Perhaps the most outstanding work has been done at Duke University, where Dr. J. B. Rhine and his associates have demonstrated that psychokinesis, the name given to designate the power of mind by which material objects are influenced, is much more than idle theory. Dice (yes, the old army type of dice used in crap games) were thrown by a mechanical device to eliminate all possibility of personal influence and trickery. Since 1934 when experiments of this type were started, there have been many tests in which millions of throws of the dice have been made. The results were such as to cause Dr. Rhine to declare that "there is no better explanation than the subjects influenced the fall of the dice without any recognized physical contacts with them." By mentally concentrating upon the appearance of certain numbers, while at the same time they stood at a distance to avoid all physical contact with the mechanical thrower and with the dice, the experimenters were frequently able to control the dice. In a number of the experiments, the scores made under psychokinesis refuted some of the traditional mathematical odds of millions to one against the reappearance of certain combinations of numbers in repeated succession.

Meditate over this for a few minutes and then realize what it means to you. Those experiments give you some idea of what is meant by "Thought creates after its kind," "Thought correlates with its object," "Thought attracts that upon which it is directed," and similar statements that we have heard for years. Recall that it was Job who said: "For the thing which I greatly feared is come upon me." Our fear thoughts are just as creative or just as magnetic in attracting troubles to us as are the constructive and positive thoughts in attracting positive results. So no matter what the character of the thought, it does create after its kind. When this sinks into a man's consciousness, he gets some inkling of the awe-inspiring power that is his to use.

Chapter Three

Suggestion Is Power

After studying the various mystical religions and different teachings and systems of mind-stuff, one is impressed with the fact that they all have the same basic modus operandi, and that is through repetition—the repeating of certain mantras, words, and formulas.

One finds the same principle at work in the chants, the incantations, litanies, daily lessons (to be repeated as frequently as possible during the week), the frequent praying of the Buddhists and Moslems alike, the affirmations of the Theosophists and the followers of Unity, the Absolute Truth, New Thought, and Divine Science.

The Bible is filled with examples of the power of thought and suggestion. Read Genesis, chapter 30, verses 36 to 43, and you'll learn that even Jacob knew its power. The Bible tells how he developed spotted and speckled cattle, sheep, and goats by placing rods from trees, partially stripping them of their bark so they would appear spotted and marked, in the watering troughs where the animals came to drink. As you may have guessed, the flocks conceived before the spotted rods and brought forth cattle, "ringstraked, speckled, and spotted," and incidentally Jacob waxed exceedingly rich.

Moses, too, was a master at suggestion. For forty years he used it on the Israelites, and it took them to the promised land of milk and honey. David, following the suggestive forces operating on him, slew the mighty, heavily armed Goliath with a pebble from a slingshot.

William James, father of modern psychology in America, declared that often our faith [belief] in advance of a doubtful undertaking is the only thing that can assure its successful conclusion. Man's faith, according to James, acts on the powers above him as a claim and creates its own verification. In other words, the thought becomes literally father to the fact. For further illumination of faith and its power, I suggest that you read the General Epistle of James in the New Testament.

Recall the panic on the night of October 20, 1938, when Orson Welles and his Mercury Theater players put on the air a dramatization of H. G. Wells' novel, *The War of the Worlds.* It was a story of an invasion by some strange warriors from the planet Mars, but it caused fright among millions of people. Some rushed out-of-doors, police stations were besieged, eastern telephone exchanges were blocked, New Jersey highways were clogged. In fact, for a few hours following the broadcast, there was genuine panic among millions of listeners because they believed our earth was being attacked by invaders from Mars. Yes, indeed, belief can and does cause some strange and unusual happenings.

Let's take an example out of the war. General Douglas MacArthur declared when he left the Philippines: "I shall return." With our Pacific Fleet in ruins at Pearl Harbor, practically no airplanes or transports at the time, and with the Japanese in control of most of the South Pacific, MacArthur had no physical evidence that he would ever return. However, he must have had a mental picture of his return or he would have never made the statement. It was a statement of confidence or belief, and history relates his triumphant return. Thousands of similar cases happened during the war and are happening today.

Chapter Four

The Art of Mental Pictures

Emile Coué, the French hypnotherapist who threw so much light on the power of suggestion, declared that imagination was a much stronger force than willpower; when the two are in conflict, he said, the imagination always wins. In explanation, let's say you are an inveterate smoker of good cigars and decide to break yourself of the habit. You grit your teeth, shove out your chin, and solemnly declare that you are going to use your willpower to break yourself of the habit. Then suddenly comes the idea of the taste of a good cigar, its aroma and its soothing effects—the imagination goes to work and the resolution to break the habit goes out the window. The same holds true of efforts to break the drinking habit and other bad habits.

Charles Fourier, a French philosopher of more than a century ago, declared that the future of the world would grow out of the brain of man, shaped, controlled, and directed by the desires and passions by which men are moved. His prophecy is coming true, yet man through his mind has barely started shaping and controlling the world.

All of this brings us to the topic of desire and what you actually want in life. There are comparatively few people with great desires. Most are content to go along filling the tiny niches in which they find themselves. They accept their positions in life as something that fate has fixed for them, and very seldom do they make either a mental or physical effort to extract themselves from those positions. They never raise their sights or realize that it's just as easy to shoot at a bird on a limb thirty feet above the ground as it is to shoot at it on the ground the same distance away. Many engage in wishful thinking, but wishful thinking in itself is without effect simply because the power factor is missing.

But when you run across a person who is "going to town"—and there are many—you realize that the great power behind it all is projected by desire. The way seems easy for those people— and to a great degree it is—because they are putting to use the powers of their subconscious minds that, in turn, magnetize, coordinate, and then transmit to their conscious minds the electrifying vision of the object of their desire.

So let's be reminded that whatever we fix our thoughts upon or steadily focus our imaginations upon, that is what we attract. This is no mere play of words. It is a fact that anyone can prove to his own satisfaction. Whether the results come through magnetic or electrical energy is something still undetermined; while man hasn't been able to define it, manifestations of thought-attraction can be seen on every hand. It is like the electrical field itself—we do not know what electricity is, although in a material sense we know how man can generate it through various kinds of energy-producing apparatus; we see electricity manifest every time we turn on a light or snap a switch.

Chapter Five

The Mirror Technique for Releasing the Subconscious

I want to tell you about something called the mirror technique. It is a method of great power. Stand in front of a mirror. It need not be a full-length mirror, but it should be of sufficient size so that you may at least see your body from the waist up.

Those of you who have been in the army know what it means to come to attention—stand fully erect, bring your heels together, pull in your stomach, keep your chest out and your head up. Now breathe deeply three or four times until you feel a sense of power, strength, and determination. Next, look into the very depths of your eyes, tell yourself that you are going to get what you want—name it aloud so you can see your lips move and you can hear the words uttered. Make a regular ritual of it, practice doing it at least twice a day, mornings

Now consider this matter of packaging in connection with yourself. Do you have eye-appeal? Do you wear clothes to give yourself the best appearance? Do you know the effect of colors and study those which best suit your form and temperament? Does your whole appearance set you apart from many who pass unnoticed in the crowd? If not, give thoughtful attention to personal packaging, for the world accepts you as you appear to be. Take a tip from the automobile manufacturers, the Hollywood make-up artists, or any of the great show producers, who know the value of eye-appeal and package their goods accordingly. When you have a combination of proper packaging and highest quality goods within the package, you have an unbeatable combination. The *you* within can do the same thing for the *you* outside—and you, too, have the unbeatable combination.

To satisfy yourself on what the right appearance will do for you, just pass by where there is construction under way. If you are well-dressed and have an air of prosperity and importance, workmen who may be in your path will step aside as you pass. Or you might try stepping into an outer office where others may be waiting to see a certain executive. Notice that the important-looking individual with the air and voice of authority gets first attention not only from the office attendants but from the executive.

No better example of the impressiveness of a good appearance can be given than the distinction made between individuals by attendants at a police station or jail. The stylishly dressed, well-poised businessman is seldom ill treated, while the man who has the appearance of a bum lands almost immediately in a cell. As a police reporter on metropolitan newspapers for a number of years, I saw this happen times without number. The fellow who looked as though he might be "somebody" and who had been arrested for a minor law infraction, often got a chair in the captain's office until he could telephone the judge or some friend to obtain his release, while the bum was carted off to jail, to get his release when and if he could.

The head of a huge automobile distributing agency told me that he was frequently called upon to close a sale with wealthy men who always bought the most expensive cars. "Not only do I take a shower," he said, "and change all my clothes, but I go to a barbershop and get everything from a shave to a shampoo and manicure. Obviously, it has something to do with my appearance, but further than that it does something to me inside. It makes me feel like a new man who could lick his weight in wildcats."

If you are properly attired when you are starting out on some important undertaking, you will feel within yourself that sense of power, which will cause people to give way before you and will even stir others to help you on your way. The right mental attitude, keeping your eyes straight ahead and fixed on your goal, throwing around you the proper aura, which is done by an act of your imagination or an extension of your personal magnetism, will work wonders.

It is always important to remember that a negative person can raise havoc in an organization or a home. The same amount of damage can be done by a strong negative personality as good can be done by a positive personality, and when the two are pitted against one another, the negative frequently becomes the more powerful.

An extremely nervous person in a position of authority can put nearly every person associated with him into a nervous state. You can see this happen in almost any office or shop where the executive is of a nervous type. Sometimes this emotional pattern will extend throughout an entire organization. After all, as has been said, an organization is only the extended shadow of the man who heads it. Thus, to have a smoothly running organization, all its members must be attuned to the thinking of the principal executive. A strong negative personality in such an organization, who is out of tune with the ideas of the management, can extend his negative vibrations to others and do great damage.

If you would remain a positive type, avoid associating too much with anyone who has a negative or pessimistic personality. Many clergymen and personnel counselors often become victims of prolonged association with people who come to them with their troubles. The impact of the steady stream of woe and sorrow vibrations eventually reverses their positive polarity and reduces them to a negative state.

To get a better understanding of the effect of these suggestive vibrations, you need only remember your varying feelings upon entering different offices or homes. The atmosphere, which is the creation of the people habitually frequenting the office or home, can be instantly detected as being upsetting, disturbing, tranquil, or harmonious.

You can tell almost instantly whether the atmosphere is cold or warm—the arrangement of the furniture, the color scheme, the very walls themselves, all vibrate to the thinking of the persons occupying the place, and bespeak the type to which their thoughts belong. Whether the home be a mansion or a shack, the vibrations are always a key to the personality of those who occupy it.

In recent years there has been a renewed interest in telepathy or thought-transference, arising out of the experiments and investigations carried on in many colleges and universities, particularly those conducted under the direction of Dr. J. B. Rhine of Duke University. The records of both the American and British Societies for Psychical Research are filled with case reports of telepathy, clairvoyance, and similar phenomena, but many people, despite the published reports of scientific findings, are prone to scoff at the idea that telepathy exists.

It has always struck me as odd that many people who profess to believe in the Bible, in which there are countless stories of visions, clairvoyance, and telepathy, declare that today telepathy and kindred phenomena are not possible. Notwithstanding the general skepticism, some of the world's greatest scientific thinkers have declared that telepathy is not only possible but that it is a faculty that can be used by most people when they understand it. In addition to the findings of both the American and British Societies for Psychical Research, and the results made public by Dr. Rhine, there are numerous old and new books on the subject. A few of the better known ones are *Mental Radio* by Upton Sinclair; *Beyond the Senses* by Dr. Charles Francis Potter, well-known New York preacher; *Thoughts Through Space*, by Harold Sherman and Sir Hubert Wilkins, famous explorer; *Telepathy* by Eileen Garrett, editor and publisher; and *Experimental*

Telepathy, by René Warcollier, Director of The Institute Metaphysique International in Paris.

When the results of Dr. Rhine's experiments at Duke University were first made public, there were many men who rushed into print to declare that the results could be laid to chance, and considerable time and money were spent in an endeavor to prove that telepathy was non-existent. Yet the experiments continue at Duke and at other leading universities. I have often wondered why many opposing so-called scientific investigators do not try to prove that the phenomena exist instead of trying to prove the contrary; but here again the writer has a theory that belief is the miracle worker, and this is partly substantiated by what Dr. Rhine himself says in his book on extrasensory perception. He declares that satisfactory results were secured when the experimenters caught the "spirit of the thing," and that the ability to transmit and receive became weakened when the original novelty wore off. In other words, while there was enthusiasm there was spontaneous interest and the belief that it could be done. But when students were called back at later dates to continue their experiments in the course of their studies, enthusiasm was lacking, and the results were not satisfactory.

I think that anyone who understands the vibratory theory of thought power can also understand why unsympathetic vibrations can be "monkey wrenches thrown into the machinery." Verification of this is found in the experiments by Dr. Rhine, who discovered in his psychokinesis tests that when a subject operated in the presence of an observer who tried to distract him and depress his scoring, the results were always below expectancy. And, contrariwise, when the same subject performed alone or in the presence of neutral or sympathetic observers, his score of successes was correspondingly high.

Despite the fact that the secretary of the London Society for Psychical Research after twenty years of investigation by its members stated that telepathy is an actuality, and the further fact that experiments at the various colleges continue to pile up amazing evidence of its existence, there are many scientific men who refuse to accept the findings. Moreover, the number of people who are carrying on investigations of their own is constantly growing, even though they are regarded in certain quarters as being eccentric and somewhat gullible. I have often wondered if those who belittle this research are really being fair, both to themselves and those interested in the phenomena, especially when the research may lead to greater discoveries than hitherto dreamed possible.

You can get the same results when visitors overstay their time in your home. When you feel it is time for them to go, simply say to yourself, "Go home now, go home now, go home now," and you will find that they glance around the room looking for the clock and say, "Guess it's about time we were leaving."

I recognize that some skeptics will say that telepathy has nothing to do with this, that your facial expressions, your bodily movements, signs of nervousness or weariness are what warn the visitor that it is time for him to leave. However, experiment for yourself; but take care that you give the visitor no outward sign, either by word or facial expression, that it is time for his departure. You will find that there are times, especially if the visitor is intent upon putting over a point or winning an argument, that this procedure will not work. But the moment there is a lull in the conversation, try it and the results will astonish you.

Chapter Seven

Belief Makes Things Happen

I have long held the conviction that various forms of telepathy or thought-transmission are used every day of our lives, far more than most people suspect. I believe that many great leaders, preachers, orators, executives, and so-called super-salesmen, some unconsciously and others thoroughly conscious of its workings, exercise the power to varying degrees. We meet a person, and before a word is spoken we experience a like or a dislike. What is it that causes the feeling to register but some form of thought-transmission? I believe that the only possible explanation of healing and affecting others at a distance is through the medium of this phenomenon, of which we are only now beginning to get a scientific explanation.

Some people have had the experience of walking into a darkened room and feeling the presence of someone there, even before a word was uttered. Certainly, it couldn't have been anything else but the vibrations of some unseen individual that indicated his presence to the other person. Evidence of telepathy? What do *you* think? It is maintained that if the first person in the room will, at the entry of the second person, think of something entirely foreign to himself and dismiss from his mind all thought of the possibility of his discovery, the second person will not sense his presence. There are thousands of people who have thought of someone, only to hear from them or see them shortly thereafter, and they have given no heed to the phenomena involved. These experiences are usually considered coincidences; but when we properly consider the power of thought, do we not have the real explanation? I cannot help but feel that anyone with an open mind and willing to read and experiment for himself, will sooner or later come to the conclusion that the phenomena of psychokinesis and telepathy are realities, and, as investigators have pointed out, that these powers are latent in everyone, though developed to varying degrees.

When we consider the subconscious mind of a single individual as being only an infinitesimal part of the whole and the vibrations therefrom extending to and embracing everything, we get a better understanding of the workings of psychokinesis, telepathy, and kindred phenomena.

In explaining psychokinesis, Dr. J.B. Rhine points out that there must be a mental attitude of expectancy, concentration of thought, and enthusiasm for the desired results if a person is to be successful in the experiments. Again we have the magic of believing at work. The subject must have a prior belief that he can influence the fall of the dice.

The writer knows that it is difficult for the average person who knows nothing of this subject to accept the idea that all is within; but surely the most materialistic person must realize that as far as he himself is concerned, nothing exists on the outside plane unless he has knowledge of it or unless it becomes fixed in his consciousness. It is the image created in his mind that gives reality to the world outside of him.

Happiness, sought by many and found by few, therefore is a matter entirely within ourselves; our environment and the everyday happenings of life have absolutely no effect on our happiness except as we permit mental images of the outside to enter our consciousness. Happiness is wholly independent of position, wealth, or material possessions. It is a state of mind that we ourselves have the power to control—and that control lies with our thinking.

About the Authors

Born in 1891 in Portland, Oregon, Claude M. Bristol worked for nearly forty years as a newspaper reporter and editor, during which time he also studied law, became an investment banker, and travelled extensively. After serving in World War One, Bristol became an advocate for the rights of veterans, whom he believed could attain success in civilian life by harnessing the powers of the mind. Bristol spent most of his adult life researching and tracking discoveries in psychical abilities and ESP, which he believed held the key to greater human potential. He died in 1951, three years the publication of his classic guide *The Magic of Believing.*

Mitch Horowitz, who abridged and introduced this volume, is the PEN Award-winning author of books including *Occult America* and *The Miracle Club: How Thoughts Become Reality. The Washington Post* says Mitch "treats esoteric ideas and movements with an even-handed intellectual studiousness that is too often lost in today's raised-voice discussions." Follow him @MitchHorowitz.

The Secret Door to Success

The Secret Door to Success

by
Florence Scovel Shinn

Your Guide to Miraculous Living

Abridged and Introduced
by Mitch Horowitz

THE CONDENSED CLASSICS LIBRARY™

Contents

Introduction
Last Testament of a Miracle Worker.........63

Chapter One
The Secret Door to Success........................67

Chapter Two
Bricks Without Straw...............................73

Chapter Three
"And Five of Them Were Wise"................77

Chapter Four
What Do You Expect?...............................81

Chapter Five
The Long Arm of God...............................85

Chapter Six
The Fork in the Road 89

Chapter Seven
Crossing Your Red Sea 93

Chapter Eight
Look With Wonder 99

Chapter Nine
Rivers in the Desert 105

About the Authors 111

INTRODUCTION

Last Testament of a Miracle Worker

By Mitch Horowitz

This book almost never saw publication. It appeared in 1940, the year that Florence Scovel Shinn died. The work of the metaphysical teacher remains a formative influence on people around the world touched by her simple message that *thoughts are destiny.*

Shinn has many times over passed the test that philosopher Ralph Waldo Emerson posed for whether someone has lived well—which is "to know that even one life has breathed easier because you have lived." I believe that Shinn, through her message of mental causation, left many thousands of people breathing easier, and living better. She may be about to do the same for you.

Shinn is best known for her 1925 classic *The Game of Life and How to Play It.* While Shinn called life a

taken the message through more "dignified forms." A problem with our spiritual and intellectual culture (and many of those who aspire to be a part of it) is its suspicion of simple ideas and methods.

Shinn's technique of "speaking the word"—of placing faith in God's channels and announcing the arrival of that which is needed—either works or it does not. If it works—and I say that, in great measure, it does and challenge the reader to find his or her own applications—where is the need for the more "dignified" works to which Fox alludes? We should never be embarrassed or warned off an idea because it is simple. The only true test of a religious or ethical principle is its efficacy. That may be why Shinn is far more widely read today than Fox and many of her contemporaries.

Shinn's natural, practical voice inspired a wide range of seekers and metaphysical ministers. In so doing, she gave New Thought its popular tone: one of encouragement, experiment, boldness, and boundless possibility. In this, the final book of Shinn's life, now a part of our Condensed Classics Library, the teacher left us a testament that conveys something of the woman herself.

Chapter One

The Secret Door to Success

"So the people shouted when the priests blew with the trumpets; and it came to pass, when the people heard the sound of the trumpet, and the people shouted with a great shout, that the wall fell down flat, so that the people went up into the city, every man straight before him, and they took the city."

—Joshua 6:20

A successful man is always asked—"What is the secret of your success?"

People never ask a man who is a failure, "What is the secret of your failure?" It is quite easy to see and they are not interested.

People all want to know how to open the secret door to success.

For each man there is success, but it seems to be behind a door or wall. In the Bible reading, we have heard the wonderful story of the falling of the walls of Jericho.

Of course all biblical stories have a metaphysical interpretation.

We will talk now about *your* wall of Jericho: the wall separating *you* from success. Nearly everyone has built a wall around his own Jericho.

This city you are not able to enter, contains great treasures; your divinely designed success, your heart's desire!

What kind of wall have you built around your Jericho? Often, it is a wall of resentment—resenting someone, or resenting a situation, shuts off your good.

If you are a failure and resent the success of someone else, you are keeping away your own success.

I have given the following statement to neutralize envy and resentment: *What God has done for others, He now does for me and more.*

I gave the following statement to a woman: *The walls of lack and delay now crumble away, and I enter my Promised Land, under grace.* She had a vivid picture of stepping over a fallen wall, and received the demonstration of her good, almost immediately.

It is the word of realization that brings about a change in your affairs; for words and thoughts are a form of radioactivity.

Taking an interest in your work, enjoying what you are doing opens the secret door of success.

The *Secret of Success is to make what you are doing interesting to other people.* Be interested yourself, and others will find you interesting.

A good disposition, a smile, often opens the secret door; the Chinese say, "A man without a smiling face, must not open a shop."

Living in the past, complaining of your misfortunes, builds a thick wall around your Jericho.

Talking too much about your affairs, scattering your forces, brings you up against a high wall. I knew a man of brains and ability, who was a complete failure.

He lived with his mother and aunt, and I found that every night when he went home to dinner, he told them all that had taken place during the day at the office; he discussed his hopes, his fears, and his failures.

I said to him, "You scatter your forces by talking about your affairs. Don't discuss your business with your family. Silence is golden!"

Success is not a secret, it is a System.

Many people are up against the wall of discouragement. Courage and endurance are part of the system. We read this in lives of all successful men and women.

Only twice is the word success mentioned in the Bible—both times in the Book of Joshua.

"Only be strong and very courageous to observe to do according to all the law which Moses, my servant, commanded thee: turn not from it to the right nor to the left, that thou mayest have good success whithersoever thou goest. This book of the law shall not depart from thy mouth, but thou shalt meditate therein day and night, that thou mayest observe to do all that is written therein, for then shalt thou make thy way prosperous and thou shalt have good success. Turn not to the right nor to the left."

The *road to success is a straight and narrow path; it is a road of loving absorption, of undivided attention.*

"You attract the things you give a great deal of thought to."

So if you give a great deal of thought to lack, you attract lack, if you give a great deal of thought to injustice, you attract more injustice.

Joshua said, "And it shall come to pass, that when they make a long blast with the ram's horn, and when ye hear the sound of the trumpet, all the people shall shout with a great shout: and the wall of the city shall fall down flat, and the people shall ascend up, every man straight before him."

The inner meaning of this story is the power of the word, your word, which dissolves obstacles and removes barriers.

When the people shouted the walls fell down.

We find in folklore and fairy stories, which come down from legends founded on Truth, the same idea—a word opens a door or cleaves a rock.

So let us now take the statement—The walls of lack and delay now crumble away, and I enter my Promised Land, under grace.

Chapter Two

Bricks Without Straw

"There shall no straw be given you, yet ye shall make bricks without straw." —Exodus 5:18

In the fifth chapter of Exodus, we have a picture of every day life, when giving a metaphysical interpretation.

The Children of Israel were in bondage to Pharaoh, the cruel taskmaster, ruler of Egypt. They were kept in slavery, making bricks, and were hated and despised.

Moses had orders from the Lord to deliver his people from bondage—"Moses and Aaron went in and told Pharaoh—Thus saith the Lord God of Israel, Let my people go, that they may hold a feast unto me in the wilderness."

He not only refused to let them go, but told them he would make their tasks even more difficult: they must make bricks without straw being provided for them.

It was impossible to make bricks without straw. The Children of Israel were completely crushed by Pharaoh; they were beaten for not producing the bricks—then came the message from Jehovah.

"Go therefore now, and work; for there shall no straw be given you, yet shall ye deliver the tale (number) of bricks."

I was told the story of a woman who needed money for her rent. It was necessary to have it at once, but she knew of no channel, she exhausted every avenue.

However, she was a Truth student, and kept making her affirmations. Her dog whined and wanted to go out, she put on his leash and walked down the street, in the accustomed direction.

However, the dog pulled at his leash and wanted to go in another direction.

She followed, and in the middle of the block, opposite an open park, she looked down, and picked up a roll of bills, which exactly covered her rent.

She looked for ads, but never found the owner. There were no houses near where she found it.

The reasoning mind, the intellect, takes the throne of Pharaoh in your consciousness. It says continually, "It can't be done. What's the use!"

We must drown out these dreary suggestions with a vital affirmation!

For example take this statement: *"The unexpected happens, my seemingly impossible good now comes to pass."* This stops all argument from the army of the aliens (the reasoning mind.).

"The unexpected happens!" That is an idea it cannot cope with.

Think of the joy of really being free forever, from the Pharaoh of the oppression. To have the idea of *security, health, happiness and abundance established in the subconscious*. It would mean a life free from all limitation!

It would be the Kingdom that Jesus Christ spoke of, where all things are automatically added unto us. I say automatically added unto us, because all life is vibration; and when we vibrate to success, happiness and abundance, the things that symbolize these states of consciousness will attach themselves to us.

Feel rich and successful, and suddenly you receive a large check or a beautiful gift.

CHAPTER THREE

"And Five of Them Were Wise"

"And five of them were wise, and five were foolish. They that were foolish took their lamps, and took no oil with them." —MATT. 25:2–3

My subject is the parable of the Wise and Foolish Virgins. "And five of them were wise, and five were foolish. They that were foolish took their lamps, and took no oil with them. But the wise took oil in their vessels with their lamps." The parable teaches that true prayer means preparation.

Jesus Christ said, "And all things, whatsoever ye shall ask in prayer, *believing*, ye shall receive" (Matt. 21:22). "Therefore I say unto you, what things soever ye desire, when ye pray, believe that ye receive them, and ye shall have them" (Mark 11:24). In this parable he shows that only those who have prepared for their good (thereby showing active faith) will bring the manifestation to pass.

We might paraphrase the scriptures and say: When you pray believe you have it. When you pray ACT as if you have already received.

Armchair faith or rocking chair faith will never move mountains. In the armchair, in the silence, or meditation, you are filled with the wonder of this Truth, and feel that your faith will never waver. You know that The Lord is your Shepherd, you shall never want.

You feel that your God of Plenty will wipe out all burdens of debt or limitations, then you leave your armchair and step out into the arena of Life. It is only what you do in the arena that counts.

I will you give you an illustration showing how the law works; for faith without action is dead.

A man, one of my students, had a great desire to go abroad. He took the statement: *I give thanks for my divinely designed trip, divinely financed, under grace, in a perfect way.* He had very little money, but knowing the law of preparation, he bought a trunk. It was a very happy trunk with a big red band around its waist. Whenever he looked at it it gave him a realization of a trip. One day he seemed to feel his room moving. He felt the motion of a ship. He went to the window to breathe the fresh air, and it smelt like the aroma of the docks. With his inner ear he heard the shriek of a seagull and the creaking of the gangplank. The trunk had commenced to work. It had put him in the vibration of his trip. Soon after that, a large sum of money came to him and he took the trip. He said afterwards that it was perfect in every detail.

In the arena of Life we must keep ourselves tuned-up to concert pitch.

Are we acting from motives of fear or faith? *Watch your motives with all diligence, for out of them are the issues of life.*

The lamp symbolizes man's consciousness. The oil is what brings Light or understanding.

"While the bridegroom tarried, they all slumbered and slept. And at midnight there was a cry made. Behold, the bridegroom cometh; go ye out to meet him. Then all those virgins arose, and trimmed their lamps. And the foolish said unto the wise, "Give us of your oil; for our lamps are gone out."

The foolish virgins were without wisdom or understanding, which is oil for the consciousness, and when they were confronted with a serious situation, they had no way of handling it.

And when they said to the wise "give us of your oil," the wise answered saying, "Not so; lest there be not enough for us and you: but go ye rather to them that sell, and buy for yourselves."

That means that the foolish virgins could *not receive more than was in their consciousness, or what they were vibrating to.*

Every day you must make a choice, will you be wise or foolish? Will you prepare for your good? Will you *take the giant swing into faith*? Or serve doubt and fear and bring no oil for your lamps?

Every day examine your consciousness and see just what you are preparing for. You are fearful of lack and hang on to every cent, thereby attracting more lack. Use what you have with wisdom and it opens the way for more to come to you.

Chapter Four

What Do You Expect?

"According to your faith, be it done unto you."
—Matt. 9:29

Faith is expectancy—"According to your faith, be it done unto you."

We might say, according to your expectancies be it done unto you. So, what are you expecting?

We hear people say: "We expect the worst to happen," or "The worst is yet to come." They are deliberately inviting the worst to come.

We hear others say: "I expect a change for the better." They are inviting better conditions into their lives.

Change your expectancies and you change your conditions.

How can you change your expectancies, when you have formed the habit of expecting loss, lack or failure?

Begin to act as if you expected success, happiness, and abundance; *prepare for your good.*

Do something to show you expect it to come. Active faith alone will impress the subconscious.

If you have spoken the word for a home, prepare for it immediately, as if you hadn't a moment to lose. Collect little ornaments, tablecloths, etc., etc.!

I knew a woman who made the giant swing into faith, by buying a large armchair; a chair meant business, she bought a large and comfortable chair, for she was preparing for the right man. He came.

Someone will say, "Suppose you haven't money to buy ornaments or a chair?" Then look in shop windows and link with them in thought.

Get in their vibration: I sometimes hear people say, "I don't go into the shops because I can't afford to buy anything." That is just the reason why you should go into the shops. Begin to make friends with the things you desire or require.

I know a woman who wanted a ring. She went boldly to the ring department and tried on rings. It gave her such a realization of ownership, that not long after, a friend made her a gift of a ring. "You combine with what you notice."

The soul is the subconscious mind, and the psalmist was telling his subconscious to expect everything directly from the universal; not to depend upon doors and channels; "My expectation is from Him."

God cannot fail, for "His ways are ingenious, His methods are sure."

You can expect any seemingly impossible Good from God; if you do not limit the channels.

Do not say how you want it done, or how it can't be done.

"God is the Giver and the Gift *and creates His own amazing channels.*"

Now think of the blessings that seem so far off, and begin to expect them now, under grace, in an unexpected way; for God works in unexpected ways, His wonders to perform.

Chapter Five

The Long Arm of God

"The Eternal God is thy refuge, and underneath are the everlasting arms." —Deut. 33:27

Have you ever felt the relief of getting out some negative thought-form? Perhaps you have built up a thought-form of resentment, until you are always boiling with anger about something. You resent people you know, people you don't know, people in the past, and people in the present, and you may be sure that the people in the future won't escape your wrath.

All the organs of the body are affected by resentment—for when you resent, you resent with every organ of the body.

I have given the following statement to many of my students: *The long arm of God reaches out over people and conditions, controlling this situation and protecting my interests.*

This brings a picture of a long arm symbolizing strength and protection. With the realization of the power of the long arm of God, you would no longer resist or resent. You would relax and let go. The enemy thoughts within you would be destroyed, therefore, *the adverse conditions would disappear.*

Spiritual development means the ability to stand still, or stand aside, and let Infinite Intelligence lift your burdens and fight your battles. When the burden of resentment is lifted, you experience a sense of relief! You have a kindly feeling for everyone, and all the organs of your body begin to function properly.

Non-resistance is an art. When acquired, The World is Yours! So many people are trying to force situations. Your lasting good will never comes through forcing personal will.

Flee from the things which flee from thee
Seek nothing, fortune seeketh thee.
Behold his shadow on the floor!
Behold him standing at the door!

I do not know the author of these lines. Lovelock, the celebrated English athlete, was asked how to attain his speed and endurance in running. He replied, "Learn to relax." Let us attain this rest in action. He was most relaxed when running the fastest.

Your big opportunity and big success usually slide in, when you least expect it. You have to let go long enough for the *great law of attraction to operate. You never saw a worried and anxious magnet.* It stands up straight and hasn't a care in the world, because it knows needles can't help jumping to it. The things we rightly desire come to pass when we have taken the clutch off.

Do not let your heart's desire become your heart's disease. You are completely demagnetized when you desire something too intensely. You worry, fear, and agonize. There is an occult law of indifference: "None of these things move me." Your ships come in over a don't-care sea.

So many people use their words in exaggerated and reckless statements. I find a great deal of material for my talks in the beauty parlor. A young girl wanted a magazine to read. She called to the operator, "Give me something terribly new and frightfully exciting." All she wanted was the latest moving picture magazine. You hear people say, "I wish something terribly exciting would happen." They are inviting some unhappy, but exciting, experience into their lives. Then they wonder why it happened to them.

There should be a chair of metaphysics in all colleges. *Metaphysics is the wisdom of the ages.* It is the ancient wisdom taught all through the centuries in India and Egypt and Greece. Hermes Trismegistus was a great teacher of Egypt. His teachings were closely guarded and have come down to us over ten centuries. He lived in Egypt in the days when the present race of men was in its infancy. But if you read *The Kybalion* carefully, you find that he taught just what we are teaching today. He said that all mental states were accompanied by vibrations. You combine with what you vibrate to, so let us all now vibrate to success, happiness, and abundance.

Now is the appointed time. Today is the day of my amazing good fortune.

Chapter Six

The Fork in the Road

"Choose you this day whom ye will serve."

—Josh. 24:15

Every day there is a necessity of choice—a fork in the road.

"Shall I do this, or shall I do that? Shall I go, or shall I stay?" Many people do not know what to do. They rush about letting other people make decisions for them, then regret having taken their advice.

There are others who carefully reason things out. They weigh and measure the situation like dealing in groceries, and are surprised when they fail to obtain their goal.

There are still other people who follow the magic path of intuition and find themselves in their Promised Land in the twinkling of an eye.

Intuition is a spiritual faculty high above the reasoning mind, but on the path is all that you desire or require.

So choose ye this day to follow the magic path of intuition.

In my question-and-answer classes I describe how to cultivate intuition. In most people it is a faculty that has remained dormant. So we say, "Awake thou that sleepeth. Wake up to your leads and hunches. Wake up to the divinity within!"

Claude Bragdon said, "To live intuitively is to live fourth dimensionally."

Now, it is necessary for you to make a decision, you face a fork in the road. *Ask for a definite unmistakable lead*, and you will receive it.

We find many events to interpret metaphysically in the Book of Joshua. "After the death of Moses, the divine command came to Joshua, 'Now therefore, arise, go over the Jordan, thou and all thy people, unto the land which I do give to them. Every place the sole of your feet shall tread upon; to you have I given it'."

The feet are the symbol of understanding, so it means metaphysically all that we understand stands under us in consciousness, and what is rooted there can never be taken from us.

For, the Bible goes on to say: "There shall not any man be able to stand before thee all the days of thy life . . . I will not fail thee, nor forsake thee. Only be thou strong and very courageous, that thou mayest observe to do according to all the law, which Moses my servant commanded thee: 'turn not from it to the right hand or to the left, that thou mayest prosper whithersoever thou goest'."

So we find we have success through being strong and very courageous in following spiritual law. We are back again to the "fork in the road"—the necessity of choice.

"Choose you this day whom ye will serve," the intellect or divine guidance.

So, as we reach the fork in the road today, let us fearlessly follow the voice of intuition.

The Bible calls it "the still small voice."

"There came a voice behind me, saying, 'This is the way, walk ye in it'." On this path is the good, already prepared for you. You will find the "land for which ye did not labor, and cities which ye built not, and ye dwell in them; of the vineyards and olive yards which ye planted not, do ye eat."

Let us say: *I am divinely led, I follow the right fork in the road. God makes a way where there is no way.*

Chapter Seven

Crossing Your Red Sea

"Speak unto the children of Israel that they go forward." —Ex. 14:15

One of the most dramatic stories in the Bible is the episode of the children of Israel crossing the Red Sea.

Moses was leading them out of the land of Egypt where they were kept in bondage and slavery. They were being pursued by the Egyptians.

The children of Israel, like most people, did not enjoy trusting God; they did a lot of murmuring. They said to Moses: "Is not this the word that we did tell thee in Egypt, saying, Let us alone, that we may serve the Egyptians? For it had been better for us to serve the Egyptians, than that we should die in the wilderness."

Someone brought her to one of my meetings, and she spoke to me and told her story. I said, "In the first place you must stop hating that man. When you are able to forgive him, your success will come back to you. You are taking your initiation in forgiveness."

It seemed a pretty big order, but she tried and came regularly to all my meetings.

In the meantime, the relative had started a suit to recover the money. Time went on and it never came to court.

My friend had a call to go to California. She was no longer disturbed by the situation, and had forgiven the man.

Suddenly, after about four years, she was notified that the case had come to court. She called me upon her arrival in New York, and asked me to speak the word for rightness and justice.

They went at the time appointed, and it was all settled out of court, the man restoring the money by monthly payments.

She came to me overflowing with joy, for she said, "I hadn't the least resentment toward the man. He was amazed when I greeted him cordially." Her relative said that all the money was to go to her, so she found herself with a big bank account.

Now she will soon reach her Promised Land. She came out of the house of bondage (of hate and resentment) and crossed her Red Sea. Her goodwill toward the man caused the waters to part, and she crossed over on dry land.

Chapter Eight

Look With Wonder

"I will remember the works of the Lord; surely I will remember thy wonders of old."

—Psalms 77:11

The words wonder and wonderful are used many times in the Bible. In the dictionary the word wonder is defined as, "a cause for surprise, astonishment, a miracle, a marvel."

P.D. Ouspensky, in his book *Tertium Organum*, calls the 4th dimensional world, the "World of the Wondrous." He has figured out mathematically that there is a realm where all conditions are perfect. Jesus Christ called it the Kingdom.

We might say, "Seek ye first the world of the wondrous, and all things shall be added unto you."

It can only be reached through a state of consciousness.

Jesus Christ said to enter the Kingdom we must become "as a little child." Children are continually in a state of joy and wonder!

The future holds promises of mysterious good. Anything can happen overnight.

Robert Louis Stevenson in *A Child's Garden of Verses* says: "The world is so full of a number of things. I'm sure we should all be as happy as kings."

So let us look with wonder at that which is before us. That statement was given me a number of years ago, I mention it in my book, *The Game of Life and How To Play It.*

I had missed an opportunity and felt that I should have been more awake to my good. The next day, I took the statement early in the morning: "I look with wonder at that which is before me."

At noon the phone rang, and the proposition was put to me again. This time I grasped it. I did indeed look with wonder for I never expected the opportunity to come to me again.

A friend in one of my meetings said the other day that this statement had brought her wonderful results. It fills the consciousness with happy expectancy.

Children are filled with happy expectancy until grown-up people, and unhappy experiences, bring them out of the world of the wondrous!

Let us look back and remember some of the gloomy ideas that were given us: "Eat the speckled apples first." "Don't expect too much, then you won't be disappointed." "You can't have everything in this life." "Childhood is your happiest time." "No one knows what the future will bring."

These are some of the impressions I picked up in early childhood.

At the age of six I had a great sense of responsibility. Instead of looking with wonder at that which was before me, I looked with fear and suspicion. I feel much younger now than I did when I was six.

I have an early photograph taken about that time, grasping a flower, but with a careworn and hopeless expression.

I had left the world of the wondrous behind me! I was now living in the world of realities, as my elders told me, and it was far from wondrous.

It is a great privilege for children to live in this age, when they are taught Truth from their birth. Even if they are not taught actual metaphysics, the ethers are filled with joyous expectancy.

So let us become *Miracle Conscious* and prepare for miracles, expect miracles, and we are then inviting them into our lives.

Maybe you need a financial miracle! There is a supply for every demand. Through active faith, the word, and intuition, we release this invisible supply.

I will give an example: One of my students found herself almost without funds, she needed one thousand dollars, and she had had plenty of money at one time and beautiful possessions, but had nothing left but an ermine wrap. No fur dealer would give her much for it.

I spoke the word that it would be sold to the right person for the right price, or that the supply would come in some other way. It was necessary that the money manifest at once, it was no time to worry or reason.

She was on the street making her affirmations. It was a stormy day. She said to herself, "I'm going to show active faith in my invisible supply by taking a taxi cab." It was a very strong hunch. As she got out of the taxi, at her destination, a woman stood waiting to get in.

It was an old friend, a very, very kind friend. It was the first time in her life she had ever taken a taxi, but her Rolls Royce was out of commission that afternoon.

They talked and my friend told her about the ermine wrap. "Why," her friend said, "I will give you a thousand dollars for it." And that afternoon she had the check.

God's ways are ingenious, His methods are sure.

Chapter Nine

Rivers in the Desert

"Behold, I will do a new thing: now it shall spring forth; shall ye not know it? I will even make a way in the wilderness, and rivers in the desert."

—Isaiah 43:19

In this 43rd chapter of Isaiah are many wonderful statements, showing the irresistible power of Supreme Intelligence coming to man's rescue in times of trouble. *No matter how impossible the situation seems, Infinite Intelligence knows the way out.*

Working with God-Power, man becomes unconditioned and absolute. Let us get a realization of this hidden power that we can call upon at any moment.

Make your contact with Infinite Intelligence (the God within) and all appearance of evil evaporates, for it comes from man's "vain imaginings."

In my question-and-answer class I would be asked, "How do you make a conscious contact with this Invincible Power?"

I reply, "By your word." "By your word you are justified."

The Centurion said to Jesus Christ, "Speak the word, master and my servant shall be healed."

"Whosoever calleth on the name of the Lord shall be delivered." Notice the word, "call:" you are calling on the Lord or Law, when you make an affirmation of Truth.

As I always say, take a statement that "clicks," that means, gives you a feeling of security.

People are enslaved by ideas of lack: lack of love, lack of money, lack of companionship, lack of health, and so on.

They are enslaved by the ideas of interference and incompletion. They are asleep in the Adamic Dream: Adam (generic man) ate of "Maya the tree of illusion" and saw two powers, good and evil.

The Christ mission was to wake people up to the Truth of one power, God. "Awake thou that sleepeth."

If you lack any good thing, you are still asleep to your good.

How do you awake from the Adamic dream of opposites, after having slept soundly in the race thought for hundreds of years?

Jesus Christ said, "When two of you agree, it shall be done." It is the law of agreement.

It is almost impossible to see clearly, your good, for yourself: that is where the healer, practitioner or friend is necessary.

Most successful men say they have succeeded because their wives believed in them. I will quote from a current newspaper, giving Walter P. Chrysler's tribute to his wife, "Nothing," he once said, "has given me more satisfaction in life, than the way my wife had faith in me from the very first, through all those years." Chrysler wrote of her, "It seemed to me I could not make anyone understand that I was ambitious except Della. I could tell her and she would nod. It seems to me I even dared to tell her that I intended, some day, to be a master mechanic." She always backed his ambitions.

Talk about your affairs as little as possible, and then only to the ones who will give you encouragement and inspiration. The world is full of "wet blankets," people who will tell you "it can't be done," that "you are aiming too high."

As people sit in Truth meetings and services, often a word or an idea will open a way in the wilderness.

Of course the Bible is speaking of states of consciousness. You are in a wilderness or desert, when you are out of harmony—when you are angry, resentful, fearful or undecided. Indecision is the cause of much ill health, being unable "to make up your mind."

One day when I was on a bus a woman stopped it and asked the conductor its destination. He told her, but she was undecided. She got half way on, and then got off, then on again: the conductor turned to her and said, "Lady, make up your mind!"

So it is with so many people—"Make up your minds!"

The intuitive person is never undecided: he is given his leads and hunches, and goes boldly ahead, knowing he is on the magic path.

In Truth, we always ask for definite leads just what to do; you will always receive one if you ask for it. Sometimes it comes as intuition, sometimes from the external.

One of my students, named Ada, was walking down the street, undecided whether to go to a certain place or not. She asked for a lead. Two women were walking in front of her. One turned to the other and said, "Why don't you go Ada?"—the woman's name just happened to be Ada—my friend took it as a definite lead, and went on to her destination, and the outcome was very successful.

We really lead magic lives, guided and provided for at every step; *if we have ears to hear and eyes that see.*

Of course we have left the plane of the intellect and are drawing from the superconscious, the God within, which says, "This is the way, walk ye in it."

Whatever you should know, will be revealed to you. Whatever you lack, will be provided! "Thus saith the Lord which maketh a way in the sea and a path in the mighty waters."

"Remember ye not the former things, neither consider the things of old."

People who live in the past have severed their contact with the wonderful now. God knows only the *now*. Now is the appointed time, today is the day.

You must live in the now and be wide awake to your opportunities.

"Behold, I will do a new thing, now it shall spring forth; shall ye not know it? I will even make a way in the wilderness, and rivers in the desert."

This message is meant for the individual. Think of your problem and know that Infinite Intelligence knows the way of fulfillment. I say the *way*, for before you called you were answered. *The supply always precedes the demand.*

God is the Giver and the Gift and now creates His own amazing channels.

When you have asked for the Divine Plan of your life to manifest, you are protected from getting the things that are not in the Divine Plan.

You may think that all your happiness depends upon obtaining one particular thing in life; later on, you praise the Lord that you didn't get it.

Sometimes you are tempted to follow the reasoning mind, and argue with your intuitive leads, suddenly the Hand of Destiny pushes you into your right place, and under grace, you find yourself back on the magic path again.

You are now wide awake to your good—you have the ears that hear (your intuitive leads), and the eyes that see the open road of fulfillment.

The genius within me is released. I now fulfill my destiny.

About the Authors

Florence Scovel Shinn was born in Camden, New Jersey, in 1871. She attended the Pennsylvania Academy of Fine Arts, where she met her husband, the realist painter Everett Shinn. She worked for many years as an artist and illustrator of children's literature in New York City before writing her New Thought landmark, *The Game of Life and How to Play It*. Unable to interest New York presses, Shinn published the book herself in 1925. She went on to write three more books: *Your Word is Your Wand,* published in 1928; *The Secret Door to Success*, published in 1940; and *The Power of the Spoken* Word, published posthumously in 1944. Shinn was also a sought-after spiritual lecturer and counselor. She died in New York City in 1940.

Mitch Horowitz, who abridged and introduced this volume, is the PEN Award-winning author of books including *Occult America* and *The Miracle Club: How Thoughts Become Reality. The Washington Post* says Mitch "treats esoteric ideas and movements with an even-handed intellectual studiousness that is too often lost in today's raised-voice discussions." Follow him @MitchHorowitz.

How to Attract Good Luck

How to Attract Good Luck

by A.H.Z. Carr

The Unparalleled Classic On Lucky Living

Abridged and Introduced
by Mitch Horowitz

THE CONDENSED CLASSICS LIBRARY™

Contents

Introduction
Good Luck Is No Accident 121

Chapter One
Chance Versus Luck 125

Chapter Two
How Zest Exposes Us to Luck 129

Chapter Three
How Generosity Invites Luck 133

Chapter Four
Turning Points 135

Chapter Five
Our Desires and Our Luck 139

CHAPTER SIX
Our Abilities and Our Luck 143

CHAPTER SEVEN
Judgment as an Element In Luck 145

CHAPTER EIGHT
Safeguarding Luck with Self-Respect 147

CHAPTER NINE
The Intuitive Approach to Luck 149

CHAPTER TEN
The Power of Response 151

CHAPTER ELEVEN
How Increased Energy Produces Luck 153

CHAPTER TWELVE
Imagination and Luck 157

CHAPTER THIRTEEN
The Luckiness of Faith 159

Chapter Fourteen
The Will to Be Lucky 163

Chapter Fifteen
Lucky Habits: Takeaway Points 165

About the Authors 169

INTRODUCTION

Good Luck Is No Accident

By Mitch Horowitz

Do you want good luck? Of course you do. We all depend, to one degree or another, on fortuitous opportunities to put our skills to use, to meet people who provide vital openings for us, and to discover information that makes a crucial difference in our lives.

You are about to experience a condensation of one of the most intriguing and little-known books in the self-help tradition: *How to Attract Good Luck*. The book offers a straightforward and ethical recipe for cultivating your ability to identify and prepare for those crucial moments where life's currents lift you, or at least help you along. The title *How to Attract Good Luck* may sound like it belongs to a gambling guide. But this book is the furthest thing from it.

Economist, journalist, and diplomat A.H.Z. Carr wrote *How to Attract Good Luck* in 1952. Carr had served as an economic adviser in the presidential administrations of Franklin Roosevelt and Harry Truman, and spent time on economic and diplomatic missions in Europe and the Far East. He amassed a great deal of experience observing how most personal misfortune arises from impetuous, shortsighted, or unethical behavior. By "luck" Carr was referring not to blind chance but rather to how we can bend circumstances to our favor through specific patterns of behavior.

In an entertaining and incisive fashion, his book catalogues the insights he gleaned on how *virtue pays*. In a certain sense, Carr's book is really a guide to honorable living, which, in his estimation, pays dividends in success, stability, and peace of mind. Carr's work is an exegesis of a statement attributed to scientist Louis Pasteur: "Chance favors the prepared mind." Preparation, in Carr's view, is based not only in rigor and study, but also in a kind of personal comportment that makes one ready to take authority or act decisively when the need arises.

In an age where people gobble up copies of blatantly amoral success guides like *The 48 Laws to Power*, I find something distinctly appealing and rock-solid in Carr's work. This is a self-help book that can be used by someone who tries to live by the Beatitudes or the Boy Scouts Code of Honor. And why *wouldn't* we want to live by enduring guides to decency and ethic solidity? Carr tells us, in effect, that we can both achieve in the world and remain appealing as people. In fact, he maintains, very persuasively, that sound behavior and achievement are intimately united. Do you doubt that? Put his ideas to the test.

Without sardonicism or irony, I wish you a heartfelt *good luck.*

Chapter One

Chance Versus Luck

People have always sought ways to improve their luck. Their efforts have generally centered around portents, omens, and black magic. The Roman augur, interpreting the flights of birds, has been succeeded in modern times by numerologists and clairvoyants. But these practices have degraded the subject of luck. At the very mention of the word, many intelligent people understandably lift a skeptical eyebrow.

But our understanding of luck can be lifted from a black-cat level to an infinitely higher and broader plane. Psychology has opened the gate to a new and rational approach to luck. Armed with modern insights, those who seek can discover the true nature of luckiness. Luck is not a mere matter of poker winnings and the like but rather a *specific condition of mind*. This book shows how the lucky condition of mind can be attained.

At the outset, we must clarify the difference between "chance" and "luck." Chance comprises the infinite number of unpredictable happenings, both great and trivial, that are constantly at work in the world, whether a volcanic eruption or a sparrow's flight. Most of the chances we perceive in life seem remote and meaningless. But now and then a chance will touch the interests of an individual—and then it becomes very personal and significant indeed. *For as soon as human emotions are affected by a chance, it has been transformed into luck.* Luck, then, is the effect of chance on our lives.

But—and this is of vital importance—chance is not the only element in luck. Another factor is involved—ourselves. For it is our *response* to chance that provides the counterpoint in the harmony of events that we call luck. Whether and how a chance affects us is largely determined by our own attitude and behavior. Chance and response, between them, provide the warp and woof of existence, and the pattern of every life.

The central theme of this book is: *We can improve our luck by making ourselves readier for the chances of life as they come to us.* Shakespeare put it this way: "If it be not now, yet it will come. The readiness is all." These words have profound meaning. For the vigor of effort that we make to be ready for luck may well be the deciding factor between a lucky and unlucky life.

It lies within our power to influence, not chance, but our relation to chance. And in that sense none of us can escape a measure of responsibility for his own luck.

Chapter Two

How Zest Exposes Us to Luck

Good luck usually strikes into the world of men with the suddenness of lightening. How can we attract this beneficent lightening in our lives?

Over many years hundreds of people have told me their stories of good luck. More than half of them had one thing in common: the lucky episode began for the person concerned at a time when he was exposed to others—*when someone else unexpectedly said something important to him.* Most of our good luck—the beneficial effect of chance upon our lives—comes to us through other people. To expose ourselves to luck, then, means in essence to come into healthy human relationships with more people. The more luck-lines a person throws out, the more luck he is likely to find.

A high proportion of lucky chances comes to us through strangers, or people we know only slightly.

This is not really surprising. Most of our well-worn contacts rarely offer us a new perspective, or a new piece of important information. But displaying "unexpected friendlessness" toward people we do not know is the secret of much of the luck of life. Ancient myths and parables repeatedly tell of rewards heaped upon someone who is kind to a travelling stranger—only to discover that the seeming stranger is a god or angel.

Of course, not every stranger merits our trust. We must guard against the aggressive bore, the gossip, or the ruthless peddler. But do not allow fear or indifference to block you off to the potential luck of The Stranger.

In enabling us to throw out luck-lines to strangers and old acquaintances alike, one quality has almost magical power—the quality of zest. Philosopher Bertrand Russell has called zest "the most universal and distinctive mark of happy men." Zest is also the mark of most lucky men—a quality which, in the struggle of life, often overshadows and outweighs serious character flaws and limitations of mind.

Never confuse zest with greed or gluttony. Zest means to take an explorer's interest in the world. The zestful person upon meeting others is curious not what they may think of him, how much money they make, or what they can do for him. Rather, he wants to discover their personalities and ways of life. He is capable of sincere enthusiasm, praise, and appreciation. The zestful person may feel angered or disquieted by events, but he loves life in all its follies. We need zest to counteract feelings of anxiety, which lay waste to human relationships.

Experimentation of almost any kind leads to zest. So does the discovery of a meaningful avocation or hobby—any well-defined core activity that stimulates thought and beckons new skill.

Frequently the things we read with zest are coupled directly with strokes of luck. Even a sentence or two, found by chance, can set off a train of lucky events. This is why books have a special place in luck development. The effort of attention needed to read a book, and especially a book with serious content, impresses it strongly on the memory, so that its ideas can be readily evoked by passing chance and brought into lucky use.

Chapter Three

How Generosity Invites Luck

Some people put out luck-lines that get them nowhere. Things may start out all right but they find that instead of good luck they have been tempting misfortune. Sometimes we reach out to people—but our *unchecked* ego gets in our way.

Probably no human frailty is more likely to bring bad luck than an exaggerated need for appreciation. This unhappy state of mind, which usually grows out of a rooted feeling of insecurity, drives its victim to advertise his importance and demand that the busy world pay attention to him. The egotist tends to be inattentive when others are talking, he causes acquaintances to take a passive position in conversation and to therefore withhold valuable information and ideas. Even more serious, such a person tends to brag and boast, if sometimes in subtle and indirect ways.

The chronic egotist is always a candidate for bad luck. But the strong characteristic opposite to egotism, generosity of spirit, consistently acts as a magnet for favorable chances.

Note that we're speaking of *uncalculated generosity.* A distinction should also be drawn between genuine generosity and the compulsive and almost frantic displays of giving which some neurotic people make.

The luck that comes to us as a result of true generosity seldom takes the form of spectacular, immediate blessings out the blue. The real reward of the generous is invisible and secret. It lies partly in their own psychological health and partly in the hearts of others—in the reservoir of good will they build up. The generous person creates an unsuspected potential of good luck that needs only a touch from chance to burst all at once into happy reality.

In luck-development we need to keep in mind this seemingly obvious yet easily neglected fact: *In order to have real friends, a man must be capable of being one.* We can, for example, try a little hard to understand the problems of a friend, and give him such assistance as we're able without seeking return. When a friend is suffering, we can suppress remarks that would only add to his pain. Likewise, when a friend is fortunate, we can fight down our envy and try to enter his gladness.

The key point is that *every act of true friendship and generosity is proof of a rising luck-potential within us.*

Chapter Four

Turning Points

It is actually possible to anticipate favorable chances. Chance, which produces the effects in our lives that we call luck, has its own way of behaving. We need to become aware of two marked tendencies in the fall of chance: *rhythm* and *interconnection.*

Chance follows the same rhythm of nature. It is not an even, unbroken rhythm. We can learn to expect the alternation of runs of chance; moreover we can learn to expect it more at certain times than others. *The runs of chance in life are normally short.* After similar chances have appeared in succession several times, we have every reason to expect a change. This calls for expectancy and alertness.

As the rhythm of chance often points to the turning points of life, so does the characteristic that I have called *interconnection.* From time to time, two or more interlocking chances in close succession touch almost every life. And it is at these points where luck reveals its power most dramatically. At such times, by alertness, we can often "pyramid" our luck, using the luck of the first chance as a steppingstone to the greater luck of the others.

It is a fact of many, and perhaps most lives, that large fulfillments come not at a steady pace but by sudden leaps. After a single lucky chance we are wise to keep all of our senses alert for other chances that may interlock with the first, and provide a major turning point of life. The conscious effort to be alert to chance seems especially productive of turning points in periods of pronounced social change, when the old order is upturned.

Enthusiasm for the spectacular and impatience with the commonplace chances of life are likely to result in peaks of good luck alternating with deep valleys of misfortune. The reservoir of luck in each of us is far more often tapped by chance in frequent little jets than in big bursts.

We must also keep alert in the face of *crucial chances*. To do so we need to maintain our physical energy at a high level. A sound regimen of diet, sleep, and exercise, helps assure the ability of our alertness and mental acuity. Beyond this, we can generate alertness through *imaginative anticipation*. Obviously we cannot anticipate all eventualities, but we can often decide in advance what we shall do if certain common chances befall us.

Finally, when the occurrence of a chance seems fairly probable, a single preparatory action can go far to maintain the essential alertness until the event takes place.

Chapter Five

Our Desires and Our Luck

There is no reason to believe that opportunity knocks only once; but whether it knocks once, twice, or ten times, only the self-knowing mind, the mind that knows what it wants and what it will risk, is likely to recognize the real nature of the chance and act accordingly. Often the claims of competing desires are so strong as to make a decision difficult. No matter how complex the problem presented by chance, a firm set of values for our various desires helps us to find the lucky answer.

By testing chances against our personal values we sometimes perceive luck where others would see none. By knowing what you really want in life, you may detect opportunities that others may not understand or value.

Here is a core principle of life: *The person who knows the relative importance, for himself, of conflicting desires is best prepared to recognize the favorable chance as it passes, and to transform it into luck.* It is not easy to prioritize your desires, but it is absolutely vital if you want to bring more luck into your life. Fortunately, modern psychology has greatly clarified this problem. It tells us that a person's desires are not fixed and rigid; rather, they are malleable, ever-changing, and evolving in us from cradle to grave.

As adults we have ten basic, universal desires:

1. Love, both romantic and the affections of friends and family.
2. Procreation, with the urge to sex, marriage, and children.
3. Group status, or a firm place in the community or group.
4. Prestige, or recognition by others of our talents and distinctions.
5. Economic security and a satisfying standard of living.
6. Self-respect, or a sense of living up to meritorious standards of behavior.
7. Self-expression, or the use of one's abilities and talents.
8. Faith, or belief in a universal purpose or goal outside ourselves.

9. Long life, specifically the prospect of long-term physical and mental vigor.
10. Good health and freedom from illness.

The evaluation of desires is a highly personal matter. Everyone has, in effect, a private blend of desires. Some want more love than others, some more prestige, some more economic security, and so on. This difference profoundly affects our ideas of what is lucky. We must also distinguish honestly between basic desires versus compulsions or obsessions. Unchecked desires can balloon into obsessions or addictions, which destroy our luck.

Chapter Six

Our Abilities and Our Luck

One of the major elements in appraising the luck-content of a chance can be expressed in the question: *Does it accord with my abilities?* Unless our estimate of our abilities is realistic, we can be tempted by chance into foolhardy and disastrous ventures.

Part of the basic formula for a lucky life is: *Make the most of what you are, and do not try to be more than you can be.* The man who tries to live beyond his capacities, physically, psychologically, or economically, invites misfortune.

The more that you know about the requirements and hazards of a given chance, the more likely you are to find good luck in it, and avoid bad luck—*if you have a realistic understanding of your own abilities and limitations.* Nothing is more promising of good luck than the chance that accords with desire and ability; nothing is more dangerous than chance that appeals to desire but is not backed up by requisite ability.

So long as your judgment is mature and sound, there is a role for *inner conviction* in assessing one's abilities. When internal conviction asserts itself with sufficient power, it can often bring luck in spite of the most adverse judgments.

In sum, only when a given chance conforms both to basic desire and to demonstrated or indicated ability does it give genuine promise of good luck.

Chapter Seven

Judgment as an Element in Luck

Judgment has been called the eye of the mind. When people demonstrate bad judgment it is usually due less to defects in thinking than to emotional factors that have clouded the mind's outlook.

An appalling amount of bad luck can be attributed to three emotional states: boredom, anxiety, and overconfidence. Use these principles to your benefit: 1) Beware of boredom. 2) Allow for anxiety. 3) Overcome overconfidence. These rules are important markers on the road to better luck.

When a person is bored he hungers for an event that will lead to a better life. He looks with favor upon anything that seems to promise a thrill. This makes him highly vulnerable to bad luck because he does not as-

lines, over which material benefits flow. For example, the courage displayed by an act of selfless honesty, such as owning up to a serious mistake and not letting others take the fall for it, often marks someone as accountable and deserving of trust with serious responsibilities.

It is never too late to reaffirm self-respect. Fortunately for us, the occasional violence we do to our self-respect *is* only occasional. A single self-respecting action, taken when the personality was in danger of becoming permanently enfeebled, can perform a miracle of regeneration.

At this point a warning should be posted. It is easy to confuse self-respect with pride—and pride is a positively unlucky trait. In contrast to self-respect, pride—whether over origin, beauty, position, achievement, or anything else—is fundamentally an expression of insecurity, with its roots in illusion. It is a sign that someone is trying to cover up a feeling of spiritual weakness by pointing to a superficial advantage or external superiority.

When we sharply separate self-respect from pride and vanity, it serves us best in the selection and rejection of chances.

Chapter Nine

The Intuitive Approach to Luck

Below the threshold of consciousness is a kind of secret reference library of unspoken knowledge and forgotten impressions. The unconscious mind at certain times will pull out the evidence that bears on a risk before you, delivering its verdict in the mysterious form of *intuition.*

Our intuitive judgments of others may sometimes arise from unconscious impressions of previous experiences with people of similar characteristics. The wife of a friend once cautioned her husband to avoid Jim, a new acquaintance at work. The friend later told me: "Jim was a good fellow, but I felt highly competitive toward him. He brought out the worst in me." The wife had demonstrated sound intuition. No one can afford to forget that while he is influencing other people, they are also influencing him, for better or worse. Getting involved with competitive people often brings bad luck.

Little mishaps in the home or office have many times been preludes to larger misfortunes. This is certainly not to say that we should seek for omens. But there is nothing superstitious about recognizing the implications of our unconscious actions. Sigmund Freud stressed this point, noting: "The Roman who . . . withdrew from an undertaking because he had stumbled on his threshold . . . was a better psychologist than we . . . For his stumbling could demonstrate to him the existence of a doubt . . . the force of which could weaken the power of his intention at the moment of its execution. For only by concentrating all psychic forces on the desired aim can one be assured of its success."

Never confuse intuition with a mere *wish* for something. Apparent intuitions that coincide with feverish wishes, and which involve high risks—such as the desire to romantically win over an uninterested or deeply flawed lover—should always be regarded with suspicion.

Chapter Ten

The Power of the Response

Some acts of chance, like a fatal accident, leave no room for response. The vast realm of luck, however, is ruled not by chance alone but jointly, by chance and by ourselves.

Even seeming disasters can be converted or redirected by a sound response, which makes us more educated, more resilient, and more knowledgeable. Sometimes the response may aid us in some other area that seems distant from the event itself.

Underlying the sound responses of lucky people to chance are three predominant character traits: *high energy, vigorous imagination, and strong faith.*

These are the "big three" that can transform raw chance into good fortune. If you are lacking in one or two of these and are willing to try to do something about it, that willingness alone is the gateway to better luck. A vigorous effort to develop ourselves in any lucky direction can itself bring us into closer harmony with chance.

We will now review the importance of each trait, and how to strengthen it.

Chapter Eleven

How Increased Energy Produces Luck

Here is a statement so obvious that one may easily lose sight of its significance: *Much of our greatest luck comes to us when our energy is high.*

Heightened energy manifests itself to us in a number of specifically luck ways—sometimes in a display of muscular power to meet a sudden chance, but more frequently in a state of mind. Notably, three psychology attitudes are closely linked to luck: *presence of mind, confidence, and determination.*

Presence of mind is a kind of alertness. As soon as we have identified the chance, the alert condition undergoes a profound change. We no longer watch concentratedly for something to happen. It has happened. Our problem now is how to respond. Instead of keeping attention focused entirely on the chance event, we

Chapter Twelve

Imagination and Luck

Wherever luck is most impressive, it is usually because energy has been directed by imagination, which reveals the potentialities of a chance.

Not every imagination, as we all know, makes for good luck. Notably, the egocentric imagination, which evokes images concerned primarily with selfish gratifications, invites unluckiness. One of its distinguishing products is the *daydream*—the fantasy that is always concerned with the future of the dream and which leads to the fictional fulfillment of some desire. Heedlessly indulged, the daydream can be a menace to good luck. It weakens one's hold on reality and reduces the energy available for the real tasks of life.

Another unlucky way the egocentric imagination expresses itself is morbidity. The morbid imagination tends to focus on the unpleasant perceptions that fit into its dark and distorted picture of life, and to ignore constructive or encouraging elements. Where this condition exists, a trivial chance can easily produce a major increase of unhappiness.

The unmistakable characteristic of the healthy and lucky imagination is that it readily turns outward, away from the self. It does not confuse the world of external reality with the images conjured up by desire or anxiety. The healthy imagination also has a high capacity for empathy, which enables you to share in the feelings of others in given situations. A great part of human luck depends on other people. When we share in their states of mind, we are more likely to respond to chances in ways that link them to us emotionally, making for a greater probability of luck for all concerned.

Just as a strong empathic imagination can bring good luck out of unfavorable circumstances, such as forming a bond with a gifted person who has experienced a temporary setback, a counter weakness area can lead to disastrous failures. This is *irrational prejudice.* Irrational prejudice includes snobbishness, religious or racial bigotry, and class discrimination. The creeping vine of intolerance chokes off the empathic imagination. What's more, prejudice dwells in insecure minds, which are natural targets for trouble.

Chapter Thirteen

The Luckiness of Faith

The word "faith" is used here, not in the sense of conventional lip service to a religious creed, but to signify the state of mind of those who are either wholly at one with their religion, or who profoundly hold a philosophic belief from which flows an affirmation of life and a moral principle.

Sometimes men and women who have neither religion nor philosophy try to fill this void in their lives by pinning their faith on their children or their work. Love of one's children and respect for one's work can be strengthening influences. They cannot, however, take the psychological place of a profound identification between the self and some large religious or philosophic conviction of good, which provides a moral basis for behavior.

When we lack the steadying power of faith, the insecurity feelings latent in all of us tend to run away with our behavior. A psychologist recently made an informal study among his university students of three negative traits: bragging, snobbishness, and secretiveness, all of which express insecurity. When he correlated the results with what he knew of the students' backgrounds and beliefs, there seemed to be an unmistakable link between the presence of these unlucky flaws and the absence of religious or philosophic faith.

We can cite very specific reasons why luck is most likely to be found in the faith-directed way of life. Faith tends to develop in the individual certain attributes that go far to ensure successful responses to chance. Courage is one of these attributes. But no less important are two traits that are in good part the psychological offspring of faith: *integrity* and *sense of proportion*.

It is through integrity that faith chiefly affects our responses to chance. Not that we find integrity in every person who professes a religion or a philosophy. But whenever we do find a person of genuine integrity, there, almost by definition, we find a core of faith. The exaltation of moral principle manifests a belief in universal law.

Together with courage and integrity, a third lucky characteristic flows from faith—the wide-horizoned attitude of mind that we think of as a *sense of proportion*. This attitude expresses itself in the personality through humility and through humor. The man who sees his actual position in the universe, and who can endure the revelation of his personal unimportance, gains enormous inner strength. Throughout life the sense of proportion links with chance to produce good luck and to mitigate misfortune.

The same quality, the sense of proportion derived from religion or philosophy, has a further bearing on our fortunes through its power in combatting envy, among the unluckiest of human characteristics. Competitive beings that we are, we all experience envy. But if envy is quickly controlled by a sense of proportion, it does little harm. In fact, a feeling of envy may be transformed to admiration and spur you to make more of your abilities. The great polar explorer Amundsen said that when he heard that Commodore Peary had reached the North Pole, his first thought was, "Then I shall visit both Poles." And he did. The danger to luck arises when envy in unchecked and becomes a permanent state of mind, which engenders bitterness, scheming, and cynicism.

The envy-resisting sense of proportion, rooted integrity, and sustained courage—those are stars of luck's constellation; and faith is their parent-quality. The need of effort to develop these attributes is too plain to need much discussion. What must be stressed is the point that any such effort, if it is to succeed, must follow the spiritual and intellectual route toward faith.

Chapter Fourteen

The Will to Be Lucky

The conscious steering of our actions, which is the peculiar privilege of man, is a skill that must be learned. The successful steersman in life, the lucky man, requires a degree of mastery of difficult arts of behavior and self-expression. Certain specific qualities of character and personality must be developed in us before we can find a lucky way through life.

When men have a keen sense of responsibility for their own fortunes, they can influence their luck far more than they dream. The chances of life, from which luck flows, are a kind of cosmic committee, constantly testing our readiness for membership in the lodge of the lucky. The *will to be lucky* is the crux of our internal development.

To modify destructive habits, which often have strong roots, *we must feel active resentment of the insecurity feelings that push us into inferior patterns of behavior*—and that make us unlucky in life. That gives us the requisite strength of feeling to challenge and change depleting habits of behavior.

Any effort we make, however slight, to prevent the dictation of our behavior by insecurity feelings is a step toward luckiness. A single modest improvement at a time is often enough to produce far-reaching consequences in one's fortunes. We have examined the importance to our luck of a number of characteristics which have a close relationship to the workings of chance: zest and generosity, with the power to attract luck into our lives; alertness, self-knowledge, judgment, self-respect, and intuition—all of high value in the recognition of favorable chances; and qualities of special significance in our responses to chance—energy, with its bearing on the presence of mind, confidence, and determination—imagination—and courage, sense of proportion, and integrity, which grow out of faith.

By doing a few relatively simple things over a period of a few months, you can often develop the lucky side of your personality to an extent that can seem miraculous. Vast and ungovernable is the power of chance; and yet, as we have seen, its influence on our luck is profoundly shaped by our own actions. The presence of this book is itself a chance, and your response to it may go far to affect your fortune to come.

Chapter Fifteen

Lucky Habits: Takeaway Points

In order to retain the material we've covered in this book, here are gleanings to consider:

- Demonstrate "unexpected friendliness" to colleagues, strangers, or casual acquaintances. In the history of religion and myth, displays of unwarranted hospitality or friendliness often prove the turning point that results in rewards being showered on someone who unknowingly aids an angel, the gods, or a disguised royal.
- Pursue topics or lines of work for which you feel zest. This is a recipe for fortuitous connections and relationships.

- Boredom is a harbinger of bad luck. Boredom leads you to rash or frivolous actions in pursuit of relief and excitement. Stay busy and engaged.
- Generosity is almost always rewarded one way or another.
- Watch for "small chances" to accomplish your aims. A small step either in conjunction with other small steps or by itself can produce unexpected results.
- Stay alert for larger "critical chances"—be watchful.
- It is lucky to know what we want. Focus brings us right action.
- Never imagine yourself more formidable or skilled than you really are. Be realistic about your current level of abilities and where they must grow.
- Healthful self-respect keeps you out of trouble.
- Avoid hyper-competitive colleagues and acquaintances. Those who make us feel competitive easily can tempt us into unlucky displays of egotism.
- Always look for how to turn chance events into good use.

- William James wrote: "A single successful effort of moral volition, such as saying 'no' to some habitual temptation, or performing some courageous act, will launch a man on a higher level of energy for days or weeks, will give him a new range of power."
- Prejudice brings bad luck.
- Ethical courage, not impulsiveness or truculence, imbues you with nobility. Defending a loved one is almost always a lucky act.
- Acting without integrity invites misfortune.
- Envy moves you to foolish actions and pettiness. It is the bug zapper of good luck.
- Any effort we make, however slight, to prevent the dictation of our behavior by insecurity feelings is a step toward luckiness.

About the Authors

Born in Chicago in 1902, A.H.Z. Carr was an economic adviser to the presidential administrations of Franklin Roosevelt and Harry Truman, and participated in economic and diplomatic missions in Western Europe and East Asia. He also served as a consulting economist to several large corporations. Carr wrote for magazines including *Harper's, Reader's Digest*, and *The Saturday Evening Post.* He died in 1971.

Mitch Horowitz, who abridged and introduced this volume, is the PEN Award-winning author of books including *Occult America* and *The Miracle Club: How Thoughts Become Reality. The Washington Post* says Mitch "treats esoteric ideas and movements with an even-handed intellectual studiousness that is too often lost in today's raised-voice discussions." Follow him @MitchHorowitz.

Printed in the USA
CPSIA information can be obtained
at www.ICGtesting.com
JSHW012032140824
68134JS00033B/3009